KOMSHE

Nikola TESLA
THE MAN WHO DEFINED THE FUTURE

A Graphic Novel by
Daniele Meucci

Illustrations and Storyboard Author:
Daniele Meucci

Text Authors:
Daniele Meucci, **Branko Andrić, Chris Farmer**

Publisher:
KOMSHE d.o.o. Beograd

Prepress and Layout:
Ivan Grujić

Kickstarter Campaign Manager:
Nevena Stamenković

Marketing and Sales:
Dimitrije Stamenković
info@komshe.com

Printer: **Zlatna knjiga d.o.o.**
Quantity: **2.000**

ISBN: 978-86-86245-48-9

COPYRIGHT © KOMSHE 2022

All Right Reserved. No part of this work covered by the copyright hereon may be reproduced or used in any form or by any means – graphic, electronic, or mechanical, including photocopying, recording, taping, or information storage and retrieval system – without the written permission of the publisher.
Enjoy the book!

For information and distribution:
info@komshe.com
www.komshe.com

CONTENTS

Chapter 1	**New York** The Interview	7
Chapter 2	**Smiljan** The Birthplace	19
Chapter 3	**University** From Graz to Budapest	31
Chapter 4	**New York** From Europe to America	45
Chapter 5	**Westinghouse** The War of the Currents	63
Chapter 6	**Europe** Back home to Gospić	75
Chapter 7	**Chicago** The Columbian Expo	83
Chapter 8	**Mark Twain** The Best Friend	91
Chapter 9	**Niagara** The Electrification of the World	119
Chapter 10	**Colorado Springs** Wireless Power Transmission	127
Chapter 11	**Hotel Waldorf-Astoria** The Richest New Yorkers	135
Chapter 12	**Wardenclyffe** Marconi and J.P. Morgan	159
Chapter 13	**New York** The Interview	171
Chapter 14	**Hotel New Yorker** The Room and the F.B.I.	181
Chapter 15	**Tesla's Legacy** Labors and Hopes	189
	Special Thanks	194

NIKOLA TESLA'S **LIFE JOURNEY**
FROM **EUROPE** TO **UNITED STATES** OF **AMERICA**

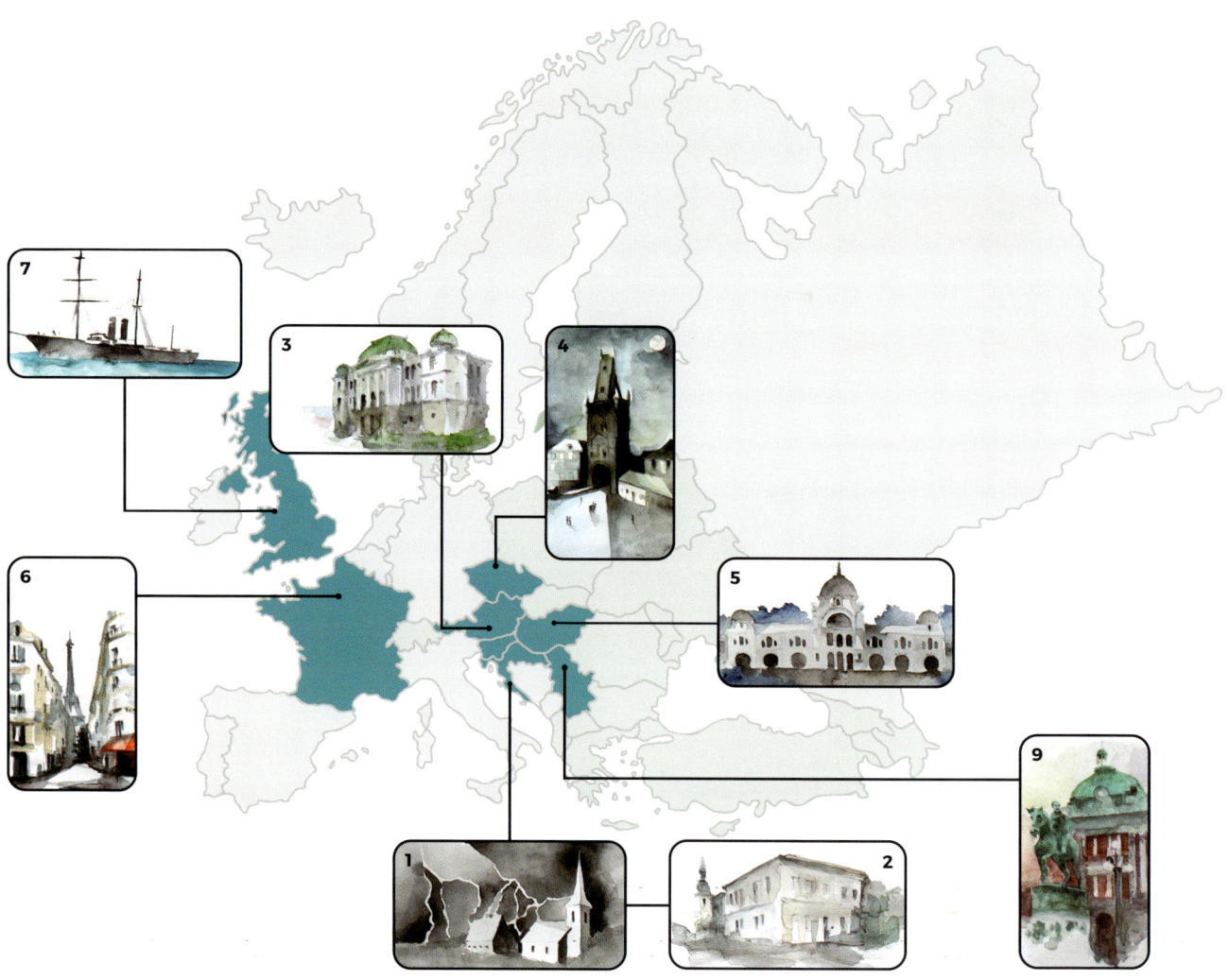

1) **1856** | **Smiljan** | 44°34'N 15°19'E | Birthplace | **Now Croatia**.
2) **1866** | **Gospić** | 44.546°N 15.375°E | Tesla attends the local college | **Now Croatia**.
3) **1875** | **Graz** | 47°04'15"N 15°26'19"E | Tesla attends the **Austrian Polytechnic School** | **Now Austria**.
4) **1880** | **Prague** | 50°5'N 14°25'E | Tesla attends the **Faculty of Physics** and **Mathematics** of the **Charles University**.
5) **1882** | **Budapest** | 47°29'33"N 19°03'05"E | Tesla has a vision for his design of the **AC Motor**.
6) **1883** | **Paris** | 48°51'24"N 2°21'08"E | Tesla starts working for the **Continental Edison Company**.
7) **1884** | **Liverpool** | 53°24'27"N 02°59'31"W | Tesla gets aboard of the **SS.Richmond** and leaves for **New York**.

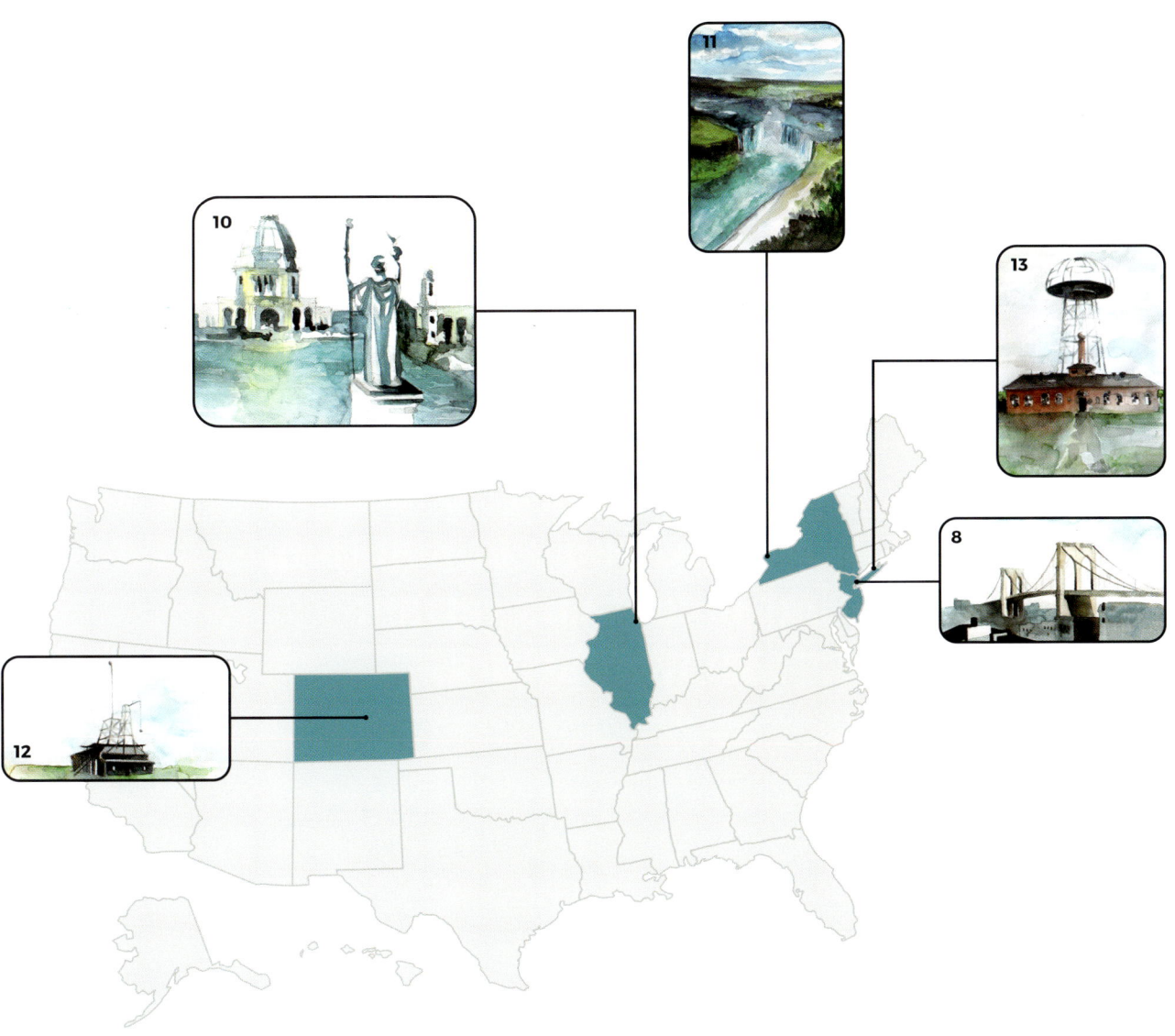

8) **1884 | New York** | 40°42'46"N 74°00'22"W | Tesla starts working for **Thomas Alva Edison**.
9) **1892 | Belgrade** | 44°49'N 20°28'E | Tesla visits belgrade for the first and only time | Now **Serbia**.
10) **1893 | Chicago** | 41°47'24"N 87°34'48"W | Tesla and Westinghouse design the world's largest **polyphase system** to power the **Columbian Exposition**.
11) **1896 | Niagara Waterfalls**| 43.0799°N 79.0747°W | Tesla and Westinghouse inaugurate the **Niagara Hydro-Electric Power Plant**.
12) **1899 | Colorado Springs** | 38°50'02"N 104°49'31"W | Tesla experiments on **Wireless Transmission** of **Energy** using rarified gases of the atmosphere.
13) **1901 | Long Island, New York** | 40°56'51.3"N 72°53'53.5"W | Tesla begins construction of the **Wardenclyffe Tower**.

Chapter
1

> "Life is and will ever remain an equation incapable of solution, but it contains certain known factors."

Chapter 2

> "What one man calls God, another calls the laws of physics."

I WAS BORN AT MIDNIGHT BETWEEN JULY 9TH AND 10TH, 1856.

I HAVE NO REAL BIRTHDAY AND I HAVE NEVER CELEBRATED ONE.

THE CLAN **MANDIĆ**, MY MOTHER'S FAMILY, WAS ONE OF THE **OLDEST SERBIAN FAMILIES** IN THE REGION.

MY GRANDFATHER, **NIKOLA MANDIĆ**, WAS A SERBIAN ORTHODOX PRIEST LIKE MY FATHER.

MY MOTHER WAS A WOMAN OF RARE SKILLS.

SHE USED TO INVENT HER OWN HOUSEHOLD DEVICES AND SHE WAS PARTICULARLY SKILLED AT SEWING AND KNITTING.

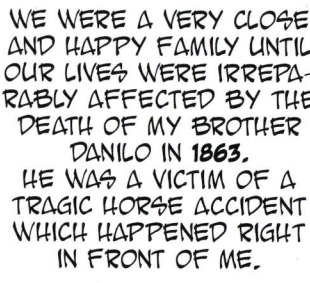

WE WERE A VERY CLOSE AND HAPPY FAMILY UNTIL OUR LIVES WERE IRREPARABLY AFFECTED BY THE DEATH OF MY BROTHER DANILO IN **1863**.
HE WAS A VICTIM OF A TRAGIC HORSE ACCIDENT WHICH HAPPENED RIGHT IN FRONT OF ME.

THIS TERRIBLE EVENT LEFT A DEEP SCAR ON OUR SOULS.

DANILO WAS GIFTED WITH EXTRAORDINARY TALENT, MY PARENTS NEVER RECOVERED FROM THIS TERRIBLE TRAUMA.

OUR FAMILY HORSE WAS A MAGNIFICENT SPECIMEN OF ARABIAN STOCK WITH ALMOST A HUMAN SOUL. WHAT EXACTLY HAPPENED IS STILL A MISTERY TO ME.

Chapter 3

> "Our virtues and our failings are inseparable, like force and matter. When they separate, man is no more."

I LEFT GRAZ IN **1878** AND DISAPPEARED FROM SIGHT.

I DIDN'T TELL ANYBODY WHERE I WAS OR WHAT I WAS DOING. IT WAS THE BEGINNING OF A VERY DARK TIME IN MY LIFE.

I BEGAN TO GAMBLE, SMOKE AND DRINK EXCESSIVELY. I WANDERED WITHOUT PURPOSE UNTIL I WAS ARRESTED IN MARIBOR AND ESCORTED BACK TO **GOSPIĆ**. FOR MY FATHER THIS WAS A GRAVE INSULT.

I WAS ABLE TO QUIT GAMBLING ONLY WHEN MY MOTHER OFFERED TO GIVE ME THE LAST OF OUR **MONEY**.

I FELT A TERRIBLE SENSE OF GUILT.

MY FATHER DIED IN **1879** AND THE PAIN OF LOSING HIM AWAKENED MY DESIRE TO RECLAIM MY DIGNITY AND BECOME A RESPECTABLE PERSON.

IN **1880** I MOVED TO **PRAGUE** TO RESUME MY STUDIES. MY UNCLES **PAVLE** AND **PETAR** (7) SUPPORTED ME IN THIS.

(7) GEORGINA'S BROTHERS.

I STUDIED AT THE **FACULTY OF PHYSICS** AND **MATHEMATICS** AT THE **CHARLES UNIVERSITY**, IN THE DEPARTMENT OF **NATURAL PHILOSOPHY**.

THERE WERE TWO PLACES I LOVED IN **PRAGUE**, THE **IMPERIAL PUBLIC LIBRARY** IN THE **CLEMENTINUM** AND THE **NARODNI KAVARNA** WHERE I PLAYED BILLIARDS AND CHESS.

IN PRAGUE I WAS ASTONISHED TO SEE ONE OF THE **FIRST STREETS** IN EUROPE ILLUMINATED BY **ELECTRIC LIGHTING** (B).

(B) THE **PAVEL YABLOCHKOK'S RUSSIAN LIGHT** EXHIBITED IN **PARIS** IN 1878, RESONATED WIDELY AND MANY INVENTORS WERE INSPIRED BY HIS WORK. **FRANTISEK KRIZIK** THE **ELECTRICAL ENGINEER** OF **HYBERNSKA STREET**, WAS CERTAINLY ONE OF THEM.

As my confidence grew the university could no longer satisfy me. I decided to quit and focus on my own work.

I moved to **Budapest** in **1881** where my uncle **Pavle**, an officer in the Austro-Hungarian army, had a few connections and **Ferenc Puskas** was one of them.

Ferenc's older brother, **Tivadar**, brought the **telephone business** from America to Europe and together the brothers established the first telephone exchange in Budapest.

I started to work there as a clerk, but Ferenc soon noticed my talents and offered me the position of **head electrician**.

TECHNICAL NOTES

AC/DC

Both **AC** and **DC** describe types of current flow in a circuit.

DIRECT CURRENT (DC)

In direct current (DC), the electric charge (current) only flows in one direction. DC may flow through a conductor such as a wire in a constant direction.

ALTERNATING CURRENT (AC)

Electric charge in **AC,** on the other hand, changes direction periodically.
The electric current reverses direction and changes its magnitude continuously with time.

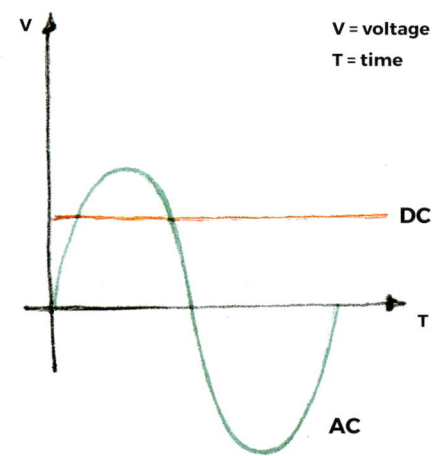

V = voltage
T = time

THE ISSUE WITH **THE DIRECT CURRENT.**

Considering that some of the current is turned into heat and dissipated along the wire (**Joule heating**), **DC** turns out to be surprisingly inefficient over long distances because too much energy is wasted along the way.
This is the reason why, to provide electricity everywhere, **Thomas Edison** needed a power plant every mile or so, covering the streets of New York with wires.

With **AC** on the other hand, we can produce **hundreds of thousands** of **volts** and solve the dissipation problem by raising and lowering the voltage using transformers at the end of the line.
The higher the voltage the lower is the current for the same power, and this principle explains why the line loss is reduced.
Fewer power plants are needed in an **AC infrastructure** and thus solution happened to be much more reliable and efficient, and consequently more profitable.

TECHNICAL NOTES

AC MOTOR AND **POLYPHASE SYSTEM.**

"Polyphase" means "many phases" describing a form of AC electrical system where multiple sinusoidal voltages exist that are not in step with each other.

The most common type of polyphase AC power in industry is the three-phase.

A simple alternator (AC generator) is a magnetized rotor spinning between a pair of electromagnetic poles, the stationary wire coils (stator windings) developing AC voltage as the spinning rotor's magnet passes by.

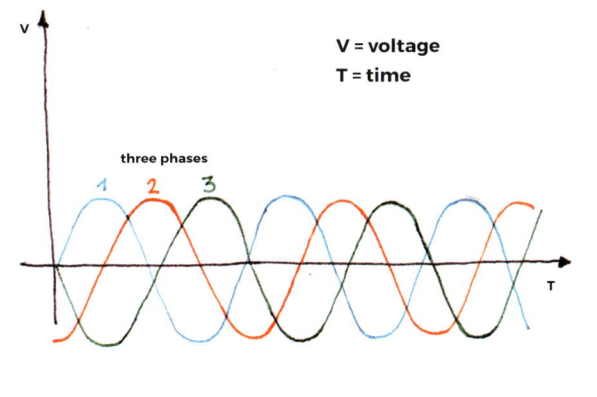

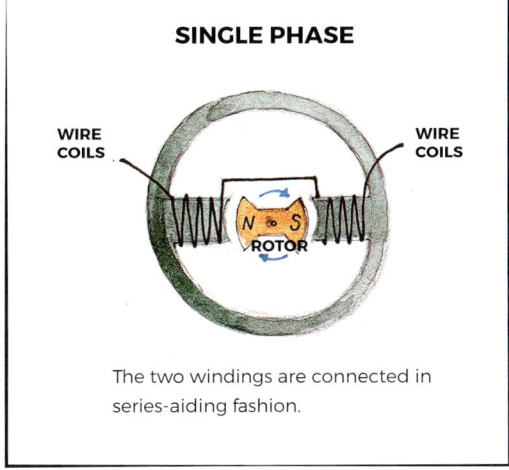

SINGLE PHASE

The two windings are connected in series-aiding fashion.

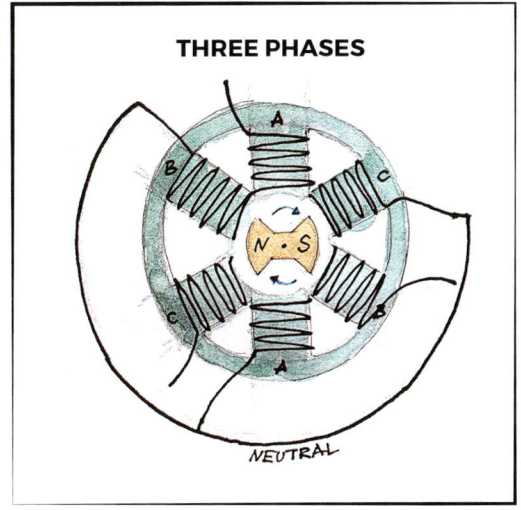

THREE PHASES

THE ROTATING MAGNETIC FIELD.

The system of coils symmetrically placed and supplied with polyphase currents generate a rotating magnetic field.

$$T = Vs/m2$$

Chapter
4

"I do not think you can name many great inventions that have been made by married men."

(9) IN 1881, PARIS HOSTED THE INTERNATIONAL EXPOSITION OF ELECTRICITY, BECOMING ONE OF THE MOST ADVANCED CITIES IN THE WORLD WITH REGARD TO ARTIFICIAL LIGHT. LA VILLE LUMIERE BECAME THE TRUE CITY OF LIGHT.

BATCHELOR WAS AWARE OF MY RESEARCH INTO **ROTATING MAGNETIC FIELDS** AND THE **ASYNCHRONOUS MOTOR**...

...AND OF MY TROUBLES WITH FINDING INVESTORS AND EVENTUALLY HE SUGGESTED THAT I CROSS THE ATLANTIC.

HE WROTE A LETTER OF RECOMMENDATION AND SENT ME DIRECTLY TO **THOMAS ALVA EDISON**.

THE ONLY THING I WAS ABLE TO KEEP SAFELY WITH ME, WAS THE **RECOMMANDATION LETTER** FROM BATCHELOR.

MY ARRIVAL IN AMERICA WAS A GREAT ADVENTURE, EVERY DETAIL OF IT, IS STILL VIVID IN MY MEMORY.

I WAS THRILLED BY THE IDEA OF SHARING MY ACHIEVEMENTS WITH EDISON BUT IN HINDSIGHT...

"WELL, WE WILL JUST SEE ABOUT THAT."

"BUT IF IT'S A JOB THAT YOU ARE LOOKING FOR, WELL, I CERTAINLY NEED CREATIVE ENGINEERS IN HERE."

OUR COLLABORATION DIDN'T START AS I EXPECTED AND IT ONLY GOT WORSE.

"BUT LEAVE THIS ENTHUSIASM FOR **AC ELECTRICITY** OFF MY PROPERTY!"

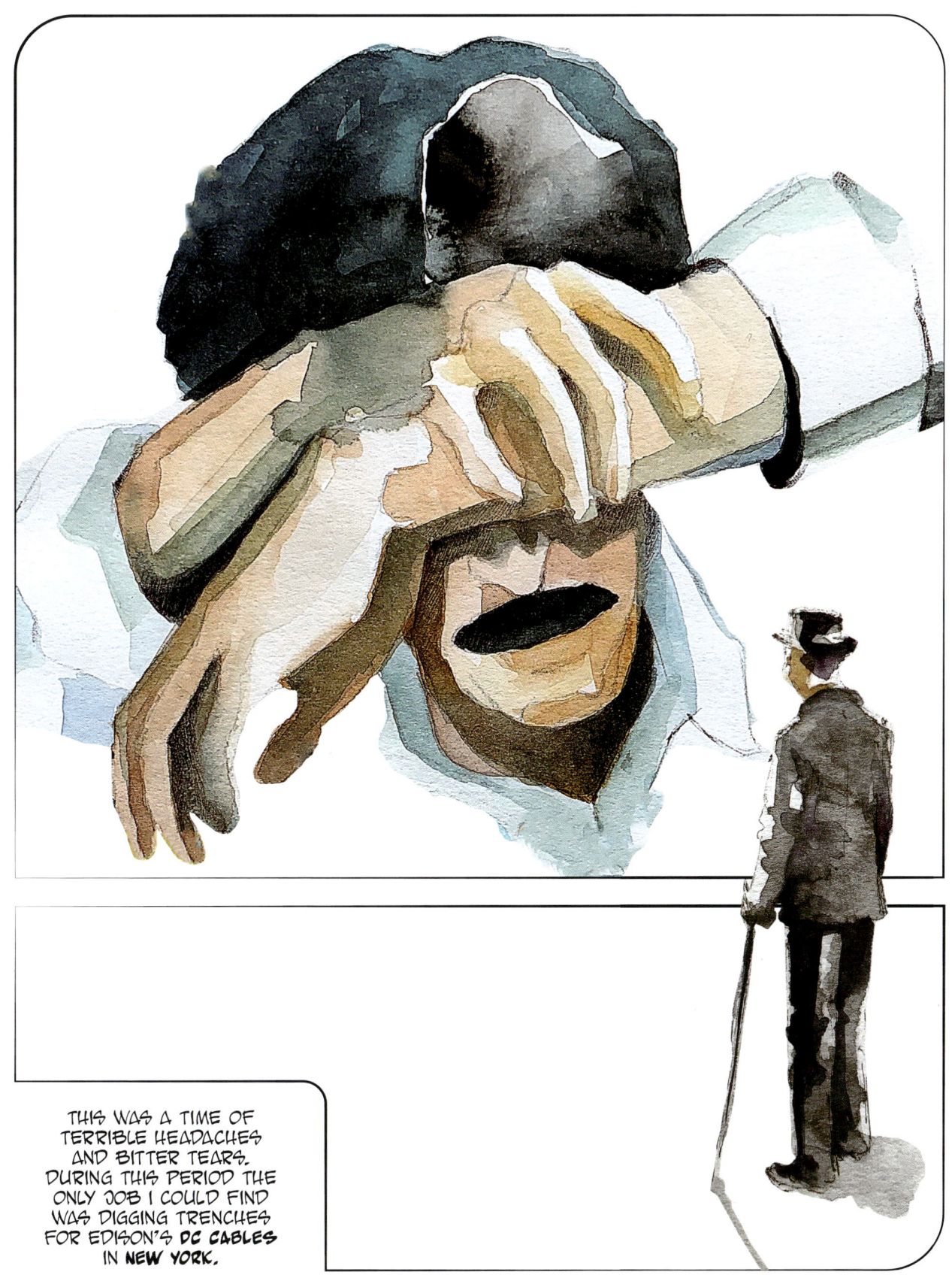

THIS WAS A TIME OF TERRIBLE HEADACHES AND BITTER TEARS. DURING THIS PERIOD THE ONLY JOB I COULD FIND WAS DIGGING TRENCHES FOR EDISON'S DC CABLES IN NEW YORK.

"I didn't give up, I was struggling to save money in order to finance my experiments."

"I am happy to finally have the chance to prove the value of **alternating current**."

"In **January 1885**, with **Robert Lane** and **Benjamin Vale's** help, I opened the **Tesla Electric Light** and **Manufacturing Company** in **Rahway, New Jersey**."

"Yes, but we should not abandon direct current development."

"There I started developing the AC generators but the investors soon left me and any further development of devices involving AC."

"Consequently I had to resign from my own company and I lost control of my **patents** registered during this period."

MY INVENTIONS GOT THE ATTENTION THAT THEY DESERVED ONLY IN MAY **1888** WHEN MY FRIEND **THOMAS COMMERFORD MARTIN**, PRESIDENT OF THE **AIEE** (11), INVITED ME TO HOLD A LECTURE ABOUT MY INVENTIONS.

THE LECTURE ALLOWED ME TO DISPLAY **TWO ELECTRICAL MOTORS**, WHICH I BUILT BY APPLYING THE **SEVEN PATENTS** I WAS GRANTED JUST TWO WEEKS EARLIER BY THE **U.S. PATENT OFFICE**.

FOR THE USAGE OF THOSE PATENTS I HAD SIGNED A DEAL WITH **ALFRED BROWN** AND **CHARLES PECK** (11) ALMOST A YEAR EARLIER.

FINALLY THE SUPPORTERS OF ALTERNATING CURRENT HAD A DEVICE THEY COULD RALLY BEHIND AND MAKE A PROFIT!

(11) AMERICAN INSTITUTE OF ELECTRICAL ENGINEERS (10) **ALFRED BROWN** WAS CHIEF ENGINEER AT THE **WESTERN UNION TELEGRAPH**, **CHARLES PECK** WAS A **LAWYER**, SECRETARY OF **MUTUAL UNION**.

Chapter 5

> "The day science begins to study non-physical phenomena, it will make more progress in one decade than in all the previous centuries of its existence."

(12) GEORGE WESTINGHOUSE JR. WAS AN AMERICAN ENTREPRENEUR AND ENGINEER BASED IN PENNSYLVANIA WHO INVENTED THE RAILWAY AIR BRAKE SYSTEM, AND WAS A PIONEER OF THE MODERN ELECTRICAL POWER SYSTEM.

WE SIGNED A DEAL FOR **$75,000** AND **$2,50** FOR EVERY HORSE POWER GENERATED BY THE MOTORS INSTALLED BY THE **WESTINGHOUSE ELECTRIC COMPANY** (13). IT WAS A REAL REVOLUTION: **THE WAR OF THE CURRENTS HAD BEGUN.**

(13) THE CONTRACT BETWEEN WESTINGHOUSE AND TESLA WAS LATER CANCELLED IN ORDER TO SAVE THE **WESTINGHOUSE ELECTRIC COMPANY** FROM BANKRUPTCY AND TO ENSURE THAT THE **AC POLYPHASE SYSTEM** BECAME THE **STANDARD**.

At the end of 1889 I went to Paris and I visited the Universal Exposition on the Champs de Mars where I admired the Tour Eiffel, which was in fact illuminated by Edison's system. The time was ripe, engineering had made giant steps and I could finally think of using big structures for my experiments.

ON THAT OCCASION I MET PROFESSOR **WILHELM BJERKNES**, THE NORWEGIAN PHYSICIST WHO REPLICATED THE WORK OF **HEINRICH HERTZ**. HE ALLOWED ME TO STUDY HIS **OSCILLATOR**.

IN THE MEANTIME, MY TIRELESS ASSISTANT AND FRIEND **ANTAL SZIGETY**, WAS IN **NEW YORK** AND MOVED THE LAB FROM **LIBERTY STREET** TO **175 GRAND STREET**, INTO A BIGGER PREMISES AND MORE SUITABLE FOR DEVELOPING BIGGER DEVICES.

> ONCE I WAS BACK IN **AMERICA** I LIVED AT THE **ASTOR HOUSE**, IT WAS A CONVENIENT LOCATION, CLOSE TO THE TROLLEY IN THE HEART OF THE CITY.

TECHNICAL NOTES

TESLA COIL

A **Tesla coil** is an **electrical resonant transformer circuit**. It is used to produce **high-voltage, low-current, high frequency alternating-current electricity.** Tesla experimented with a number of different configurations consisting of two, or sometimes three, coupled **resonant electric circuits**.

Tesla used these circuits to conduct innovative experiments in **electrical lighting, phosphorescence, X-ray generation, high frequency alternating current phenomena, electrotherapy,** and **the transmission of electrical energy without wires**. Tesla coil circuits were used commercially in **sparkgap radio transmitters** for **wireless telegraphy** until the 1920s, and in **medical equipment** such as **electrotherapy** and **violet ray** devices.

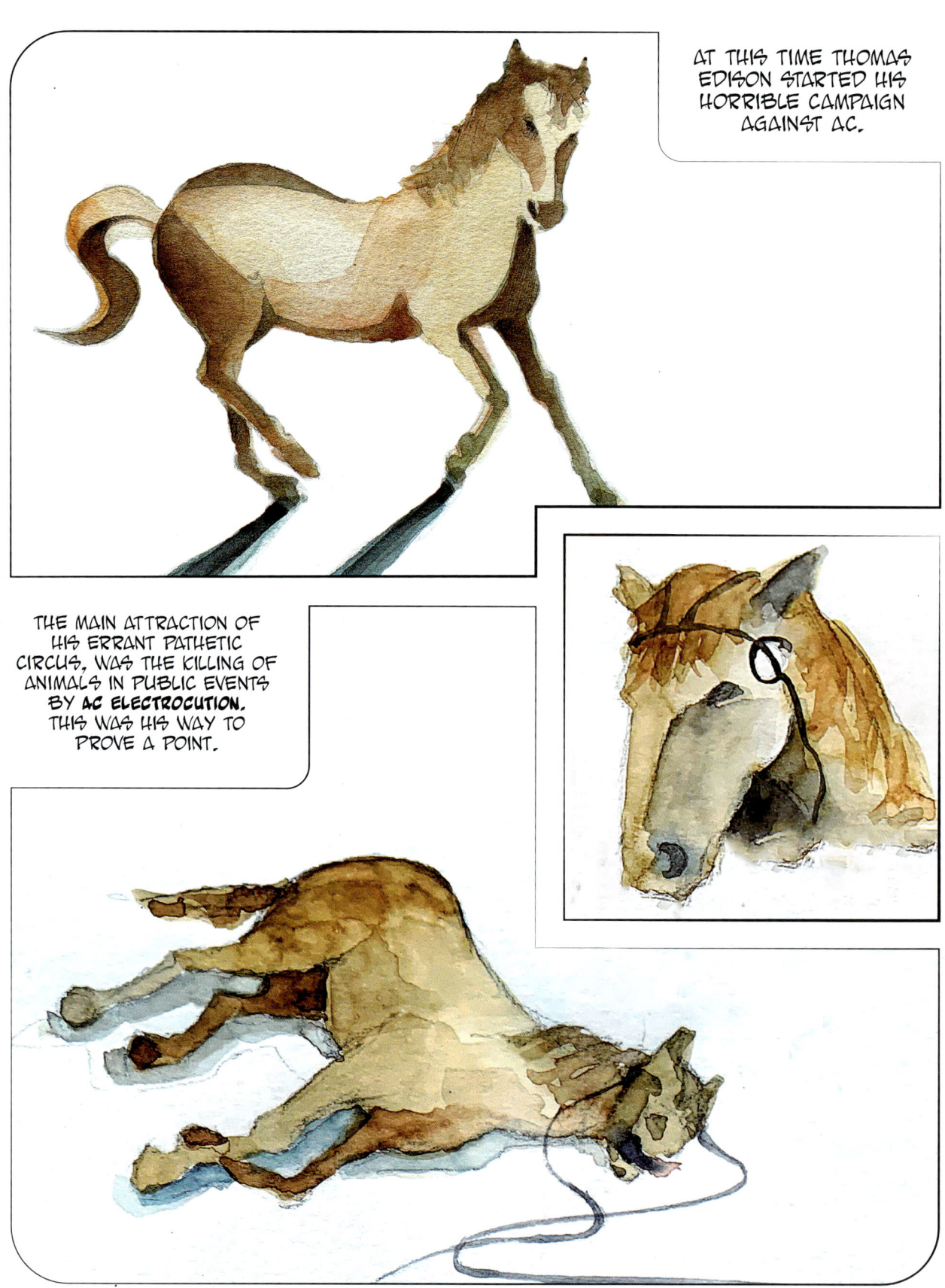

> JUST A FEW YEARS LATER THEY GAVE THE SAME TREATMENT TO **WILLIAM KEMMLER (14)**. ALTHOUGH HE WAS GUILTY, THIS WAS A SHOCKINGLY CRUEL WAY TO DIE.

(14) **WILLIAM KEMMLER** WAS AN AMERICAN PEDDLER, ALCOHOLIC, AND MURDERER, WHO, IN **1890**, BECAME THE FIRST PERSON IN THE WORLD TO BE EXECUTED BY **ELECTRIC CHAIR**. HE WAS CONVICTED OF MURDERING HIS WIFE **MATILDA "TILLIE" ZIEGLER**, TWO YEARS EARLIER. ALTHOUGH ELECTROCUTION HAD PREVIOUSLY BEEN SUCCESSFULLY USED TO KILL A HORSE, KEMMLER'S EXECUTION DID NOT GO SMOOTHLY.

Chapter 6

> "Be alone, that is the secret of invention; be alone, that is when ideas are born."

ONCE I RECEIVED MY **AMERICAN CITIZENSHIP** ON **JULY 30TH 1891**, I STARTED TOURING EUROPE AND GIVING LECTURES IN MAJOR UNIVERSITIES DURING THE FOLLOWING YEAR (1892).

Chapter 7

> "The present is theirs; the future, for which I really worked, is mine."

OUR SUCCESS AT THE **COLUMBIAN EXPOSITION** IN **CHICAGO** SIGNALED THE END OF THE WAR OF THE CURRENTS. TO POWER THE **180,000 LIGHTBULBS** I BUILT THE **WORLD'S LARGEST POLYPHASE SYSTEM** (16) AT THE TIME.

(16) WHEN THE **1893 CHICAGO WORLD FAIR** WAS ILLUMINATED USING NIKOLA TESLA'S INVENTIONS FOR A/C ELECTRICITY AND FLUORESCENT LIGHTING, IT WAS A SPECTACLE THAT AMAZED THE WORLD. IT WAS THE TESLA'S VICTORY OVER EDISON IN THE WAR OF THE CURRENTS. TESLA PROVED TO THE WORLD THAT **AC** WAS SUPERIOR TO **DC** FOR SAFELY TRANSMITTING POWER OVER LONG DISTANCES, AND **AC** BECAME THE **STANDARD SYSTEM** OF OUR MODERN POWER SYSTEM.

On **May 1st, 1893**, the **U.S. President Grover Cleveland** inaugurated the fair by pressing a golden button and lit **thousands of lightbulbs**.

25 million Americans finally saw the potential of **alternating current**.

DURING THE FAIR I DISPLAYED A **NEW RANGE OF LIGHT BULBS WITH RAREFIED GASES** AND...

...THE **EGG OF COLUMBUS**, A DEVICE THAT SHOWS THE ROTATING MAGNETIC FIELD GENERATED BY MY **AC INDUCTION MOTORS**.

ONCE THE **AC MOTOR** IS POWERED BY A **TWO PHASE AC SOURCE**, IT GENERATES A **ROTATING MAGNETIC FIELD**, WHICH INDUCES THE **COPPER EGG** PLACED ON THE TOP PART, TO SPIN DUE TO **GYROSCOPIC ACTION**.

(17) THREE ELEMENTARY CONCEPTS OF THE **VEDANTIC DOCTRINE**. **PRANA** MIGHT BE UNDERSTOOD AS A UNIT OF **ENERGY**, **AKASHA** AS **MATTER**, AND **KALPAS** AS **TIME**. ACCORDING TO **VIVEKANANDA**, TESLA ASSURED HIM THAT IDEAS OF SUCH A LONG TRADITION IN **HINDUISM** COULD FIND AN ECHO IN **MODERN SCIENCE**.

Chapter
8

"If you only knew the magnificence of the 3, 6 and 9, then you would have the key to the universe."

FOLLOWING THE EXPO I STARTED TO FOCUS MORE ON **HIGH FREQUENCY DEVICES** AND THE DEVELOPMENT OF **WIRELESS COMMUNICATION** (18).

(18) CONDUCTING MANY EXPERIMENTS USING HIS **TESLA COILS**, THE INVENTOR SOON DISCOVERED THAT HE COULD TRANSMIT AND RECEIVE POWERFUL RADIO SIGNALS WHEN HIS DEVICES WERE TUNED TO RESONATE AT THE SAME FREQUENCY.

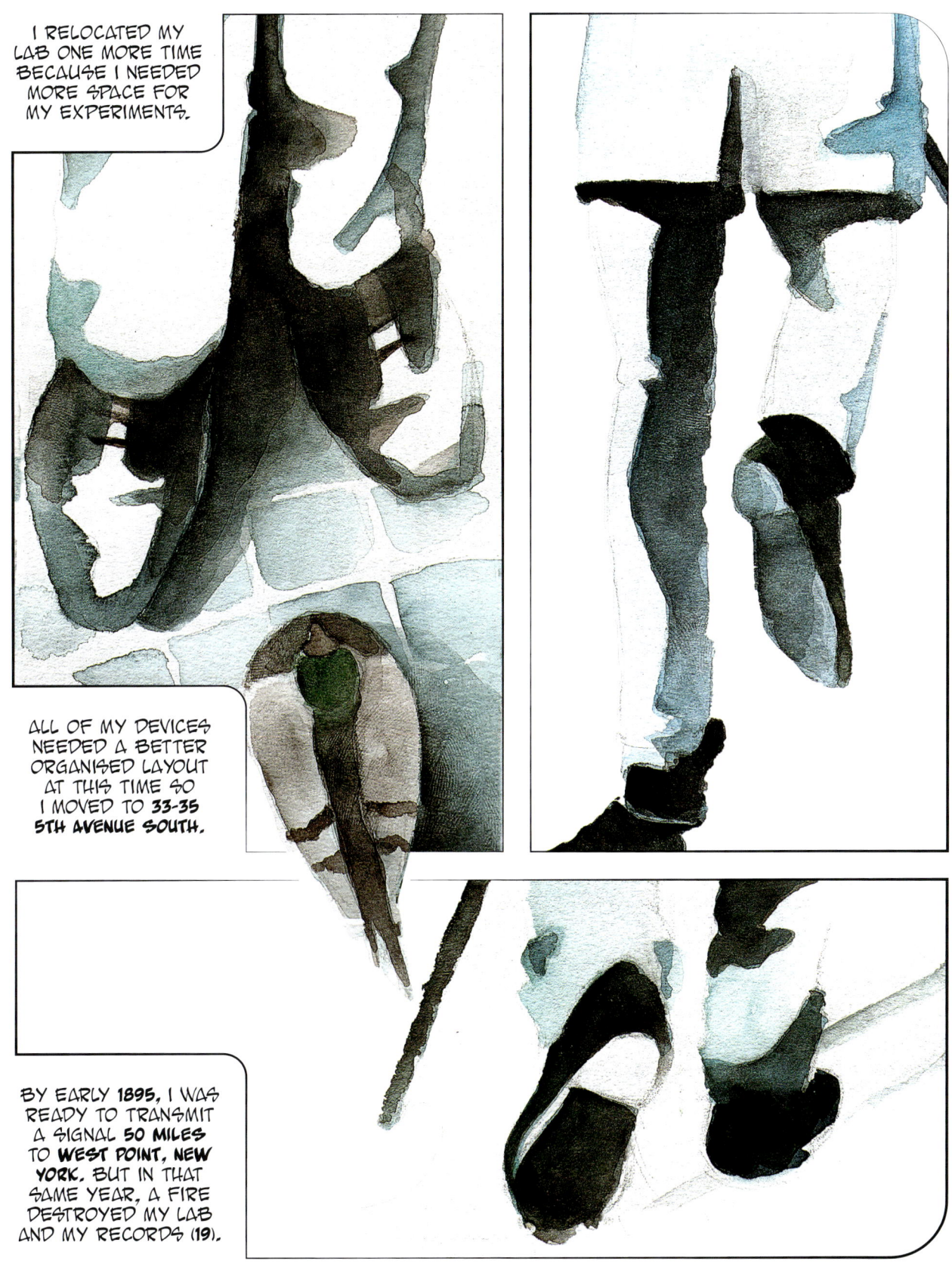

I RELOCATED MY LAB ONE MORE TIME BECAUSE I NEEDED MORE SPACE FOR MY EXPERIMENTS.

ALL OF MY DEVICES NEEDED A BETTER ORGANISED LAYOUT AT THIS TIME SO I MOVED TO **33-35 5TH AVENUE SOUTH.**

BY EARLY **1895**, I WAS READY TO TRANSMIT A SIGNAL **50 MILES** TO **WEST POINT, NEW YORK.** BUT IN THAT SAME YEAR, A FIRE DESTROYED MY LAB AND MY RECORDS (19).

(19) THE TIMING COULD NOT HAVE BEEN WORSE. IN THE SAME PERIOD IN **ENGLAND**, A YOUNG ITALIAN INVENTOR NAMED **GUGLIELMO MARCONI** WAS DEVELOPING A DEVICE FOR **WIRELESS TELEGRAPHY.**

(20) AT DELMONICO'S TESLA USED TO ATTEND FORMAL AND INFORMAL EVENTS AND MEETINGS. THERE HE WAS SURROUNDED BY POPULAR NEW YORKERS, INVESTORS, ARTISTS, TRADERS AND FAMOUS FIGURES WHO BECAME CLOSE FRIENDS SUCH AS MARK TWAIN.

THIS TIME I RENTED THE WHOLE **4TH FLOOR** OF THE BUILDING.

I WAS CONSTANTLY WORKING, SOMETIMES WITHOUT A BREAK FOR SEVERAL DAYS.

OFTEN I HAD GUESTS VISIT ME LATE AT NIGHT, WHOM I ENTERTAINED WITH SOME OF MY DEMONSTRATIONS.

MARK TWAIN AND ROBERT U. JOHNSON (21) OFTEN ENJOYED SPENDING TIME WITH ME.

(21) **SAMUEL LANGHORNE CLEMENS** KNOWN BY HIS PEN NAME **MARK TWAIN**, WAS AN AMERICAN WRITER, HUMORIST, ENTREPRENEUR, PUBLISHER, AND LECTURER. **ROBERT UNDERWOOD JOHNSON** WAS AN AMERICAN WRITER, POET, AND DIPLOMAT.

ROBERT, WHO WAS THE EDITOR OF THE **CENTURY MAGAZINE** IN THAT PERIOD, PUBLISHED SOME OF MY ARTICLES AND EXTRACTS FROM MARK'S BOOKS. WE WERE CLOSE FRIENDS.

YOU ARE SHOWING ME MAGIC SUCH AS I HAVE NEVER SEEN! AND I HAVE SEEN A FEW THINGS!

RIGHT NOW ONLY A FEW UNDERSTAND WHAT MY WORK COULD MEAN.

A NEW INVENTION ENCOMPASSES YOUR VERY BEING AND PUSHES YOU INTO THE UNKNOWN.

Chapter 9

"The individual is ephemeral, races and nations come and pass away, but man remains."

"LA LIBERTÉ ÉCLAIRANT LE MONDE" IS ITS REAL NAME IN FRENCH, WHILE IN ENGLISH IT WOULD BE "**THE LIBERTY LIGHTING THE WORLD.**"

"GIVE ME YOUR TIRED, YOUR POOR, YOUR HUDDLED MASSES YEARNING TO BREATHE FREE, THE WRETCHED REFUSE OF YOUR TEEMING SHORE" (22).

(22) AT THE BASE OF THE COPPER STATUE A TABLET IS INSCRIBED WITH WORDS PENNED BY **EMMA LAZARUS** IN **1883**. THE STATUE IS A GIFT FROM THE PEOPLE OF FRANCE TO THE PEOPLE OF THE UNITED STATES. THE STATUE WAS DESIGNED BY FRENCH SCULPTOR **FREDERIC AUGUSTE BARTHOLDI** AND ITS METAL FRAMEWORK WAS BUILT BY **GUSTAVE EIFFEL**. THE STATUE WAS INAUGURATED ON **28TH OCTOBER, 1886**.

THIS GREAT SUCCESS CAME JUST **3 YEARS** AFTER THE **CHICAGO FAIR**.

THE ELECTRIFICATION OF THE WORLD HAD BEGUN.

THIS TECHNOLOGY SPREAD WORLDWIDE SO QUICKLY THAT EVEN ISOLATED SMALL TOWNS BEGAN TO HAVE LIGHT AND ELECTRICITY IN LESS THAN A DECADE (23).

(23) WHEN ON **SAINT NIKOLA'S DAY** IN 1911 THE **IVANJICA HYDROPOWER PLANT** OPENED, IT WAS ALREADY THE **SEVENTH HYDROPOWER PLANT** IN THE TERRITORY OF CURRENT **SERBIA**.

TECHNICAL NOTES

NIAGARA POWER PLANT.

The **Adams Power Plant Transformer House** in **Niagara Falls,** built by **Nikola Tesla** and **George Westinghouse** in **1895,** was the first **hydro-electric power plant** and begun the process of **electrifying the world.**
It was equipped with **ten 5,000-horsepower Tesla/Westinghouse AC generators.**

The **electrical power** generated by processing the **gravitational force** caused by **falling** or **flowing water** is called **Hydroelectricity**.
In this case, the source of the flowing or falling water is **Niagara Falls,** and this wasn't a new thought for Tesla as he had always dreamed of generating energy by controlling the forces of nature.

The Power Plant was named after **Edward Dean Adams, President** of the **Cataract Construction Company,** the American company that funded the project.
The **CCC** put together a team of experts to pick the best way to harness the mechanical energy of the **Niagara River** for industrial use.
This group of experts gathered under the name of **International Niagara Commission** which was led by a charismatic British mathematician, physicist and engineer, **William Thomson, 1st Baron Kelvin,** who did important work in the mathematical analysis of electricity and formulation of the **first** and **second laws** of **thermodynamics**.

Chapter 10

"If you want to find the secrets of the universe, think in terms of energy, frequency and vibration."

DURING THE **ELECTRICAL EXHIBITION** IN **1898** AT **MADISON SQUARE GARDEN** I STAGED A DEMONSTRATION COMPLETELY BEYOND THE GENERALLY ACCEPTED LIMITS OF TECHNOLOGY.

I DISPLAYED A **RADIO REMOTE CONTROLLED BOAT**, AN INVENTION THAT I PATENTED AS A "**METHOD OF AND APPARATUS FOR CONTROLLING MECHANISM OF MOVING VESSELS OR VEHICLES**".

THIS INVENTION DEMONSTRATED THE AMAZING APPLICATION OF **RADIO TECHNOLOGY** AND THAT **RADIO COMMUNICATION** WAS ALREADY THERE MUCH BEFORE **MARCONI**.

Chapter 11

> "A new idea must not be judged by its immediate results."

(24) NIKOLA TESLA WOULD EVENTUALLY BE ASKED TO LEAVE THE HOTEL WALDORF-ASTORIA FOR NOT PAYING HIS BILLS.

(25) **GEORGE KARL BOLDT** WAS A PRUSSIAN-AMERICAN HOTELIER. A SELF-MADE MILLIONAIRE, HE INFLUENCED THE DEVELOPMENT OF THE URBAN HOTEL AS A CIVIC SOCIAL CENTER AND LUXURY DESTINATION.

Panel 1:
"NIKOLA! WE MUST SET AN APPOINTMENT FOR THAT INTERVIEW FOR THE **CENTURY** MAGAZINE."

Panel 2:
"WHAT YOU SHOWED ME AT THE LAB WAS FASCINATING."

THE **EMPIRE ROOM** WAS THE LARGEST MOST ADORNED ROOM OF THE **WALDORF-ASTORIA**.

(27) ANNE MORGAN, AMERICAN PHILANTROPIST DAUGHTER OF THE FAMOUS FINANCIER AND BANKER J.P. MORGAN.

"Do you need more napkins, sir (28)?"

(28) **NIKOLA TESLA** HAD THE HABIT OF SHINING HIS OWN CUTLERY AND DISHES WITH 3 NAPKINS EACH FOR A TOTAL OF **18 NAPKINS**.

"Sweetheart, don't bother Mr. Tesla with your strange ideas."

"Please consider it, I will be back in **New York** in 3 weeks."

"I WOULD LIKE TO THANK ALL OF YOU FOR COMING TO THE CLUB TODAY."

AT THE CLUB THE ENGINEERS HAD THE OPPORTUNITY TO SHARE THEIR INVENTIONS AND DISCUSS TECHNICAL TOPICS WITH OTHER ENGINEERS AND INVENTORS.

"TONIGHT WE WILL HAVE AN OPPORTUNITY TO HEAR ABOUT THE LATEST IMPROVEMENTS IN **AC TECHNOLOGY** FROM **MR. TESLA**."

(31) **MARCONI** WAS BORN INTO THE **ITALIAN NOBILITY** IN **PALAZZO MARESCALCHI** IN **BOLOGNA** ON **25TH APRIL 1874**. HE WAS THE SECOND SON OF **GIUSEPPE MARCONI** (AN ITALIAN ARISTOCRATIC LANDOWNER FROM **PORRETTA TERME**) AND HIS **IRISH** WIFE **ANNIE JAMESON** (DAUGHTER OF **ANDREW JAMESON** OF **DAPHNE CASTLE** IN **COUNTY WEXFORD, IRELAND**, AND GRANDDAUGHTER OF **JOHN JAMESON**, FOUNDER OF **WHISKEY DISTILLERS JAMESON & SONS**).

"VERY GOOD, HOW ARE YOU MIHAJLO?"

AT THIS POINT WE HAD NOT SEEN EACH OTHER FOR 3 DECADES, EVER SINCE HE SUPPORTED **MARCONI** DURING THE TRIAL FOR THE **RADIO PATENT**.

MARCONI LEARNT EVERYTHING FROM ME WHILE WORKING AS MY ASSISTANT.

DURING THE TRIAL **PUPIN** SERVED AS A WITNESS AND HE GAVE TESTIMONY IN FAVOR OF **MARCONI** BECAUSE HE HAD ALREADY SIGNED AN AGREEMENT WITH HIM. HE ALSO PUBLICLY QUESTIONED MY MENTAL HEALTH THUS COMPROMISING MY CAREER.

BUT I DON'T HOLD IT AGAINST HIM, WE ARE BOTH OLD MEN AND ESPECIALLY SINCE I HEARD THAT MIHAJLO IS SUFFERING WITH POOR HEALTH **(33)**.

(33) ON HIS DEATH BED IN **MARCH 1935**, PUPIN EXPRESSED A DESIRE TO SAY FAREWELL TO TESLA THROUGH **CONSUL JANKOVIC**. THEY SPENT HALF AN HOUR ALONE BUT PUPIN WASN'T ABLE TO SPEAK ANYMORE. TESLA NEVER REVEALED THE CONTENTS OF THEIR LAST MEETING. **MIHAJLO PUPIN** DIED JUST 40 HOURS AFTER THEIR MEETING ON **12TH MARCH 1935**, A MONTH AFTER NIKOLA TESLA'S INTERVIEW WITH **VIERECK**.

Chapter 12

> "I don't care that they stole my idea. I care that they don't have any of their own."

MY TROUBLE WITH **MARCONI** STARTED WHEN I SIGNED OVER **51%** OF THE **INTERESTS** IN MY **PATENTS** TO **J.P. MORGAN** FOR ONLY **$150,000**. I USED THIS MONEY FOR MY MOST CHALLENGING PROJECT: THE **WARDENCLYFFE TOWER**.

FOCUS ON THESE TWO WORDS MR. TESLA: **WIRELESS COMMUNICATION**. THIS IS WHAT WE HAVE TO ACHIEVE.

MORGAN FINANCED THE PROJECT WITH THE GOAL OF DESIGNING AN EFFICIENT **RADIO SYSTEM TECHNOLOGY** FOR **SENDING MESSAGES OVER LONG DISTANCES**. MY PLAN INSTEAD, WAS EVEN MORE EXCITING. I WANTED TO PROVIDE **WIRELESS POWER WORLDWIDE**, BY FOLLOWING THE SAME PRINCIPLES.

TO ACHIEVE OUR GOALS WE BUILT THE **WARDENCLYFFE TOWER**, **87 METERS HIGH** (34). IN THIS LAB I PLACED THE BIGGEST OSCILLATOR I HAVE EVER DESIGNED.

(34) THE TOWER WAS DEMOLISHED IN 1917 AND THE PROPERTY WAS SOLD IN AN ATTEMPT TO PAY THE BILLS THAT TESLA HAD AT **WALDORF-ASTORIA**.

IN THE MEANTIME **MARCONI** WAS CONDUCTING HIS EXPERIMENTS ON **RADIO COMMUNICATION** ABOARD OF HIS **STEAM YATCH** ELETTRA.

I MUST ADMIT THAT I UNDERESTIMATED THE ITALIAN, BUT ALSO I WASN'T REALLY BOTHERED BY THE FACT THAT HE WAS USING **17 OF MY PATENTS** TO PUT TOGETHER A **COMMUNICATION DEVICE**.

IN 1909 MARCONI RECEIVED THE **NOBEL PRIZE** FOR PHYSICS (35). IT WAS VERY DISAPPOINTING.

(35) IN 1909 THE **NOBEL PRIZE** FOR PHYSICS WAS SHARED BETWEEN GUGLIELMO MARCONI AND KARL FERDINAND BRAUN "IN RECOGNITION OF THEIR CONTRIBUTION TO THE DEVELOPMENT OF WIRELESS TELEGRAPHY". NIKOLA TESLA WAS VERY DISAPPOINTED BY THIS NEWS BECAUSE HE WAS CERTAINLY THE FATHER OF RADIO TECHNOLOGY.

I WAS PROUD HOWEVER THAT **MARCONI'S WORK** ALLOWED FOR OVER SEVEN HUNDRED PASSENGERS TO BE RESCUED (36).

(36) THE **TITANIC** WAS ONE OF THE **FIRST SHIPS** WITH AN **ONBOARD RADIO COMMUNICATION SYSTEM**. MARCONI'S INTUITION TO USE THE TECHNOLOGY ON SHIPS WAS VITAL IN THE RESCUE OF TITANIC'S PASSENGERS. THE **SOS MESSAGE** SENT FROM THE TITANIC A FEW MINUTES AFTER MIDNIGHT ON **15TH OF APRIL 1912** WAS RECEIVED BY THE SHIP **RMS CARPATHIA**, WHICH WAS TRAVELLING FROM **NEW YORK** TO **RIJEKA (NOW CROATIA)**. THE CREW WAS ABLE TO RESCUE OVER **SEVEN HUNDRED PASSENGERS** AND ENTER THE **NEW YORK HARBOUR** ON THE EVENING OF **18TH OF APRIL**. THIS MOMENT DEMONSTRATED THE IMPORTANCE OF MARCONI'S RADIO COMMUNICATION DEVICE FOR **NAVIGATIONAL PURPOSES**. HE WAS RIGHTLY CELEBRATED FOR THIS ACHIEVEMENT.

Chapter 13

> "You may live to see man-made horrors beyond your comprehension."

THE DEATH RAY.

IT WILL SEND CONCENTRATED BEAMS OF PARTICLES THROUGH THE AIR, WITH SUCH TREMENDOUS ENERGY THAT THEY WILL BRING DOWN A FLEET OF **10,000 ENEMY AIRPLANES** AT A DISTANCE OF **250 MILES**.

THE BORDERS OF EVERY COUNTRY WILL BE SURROUNDED BY THIS DEFENSE SYSTEM AND WAR AS WE KNOW IT WILL BE SIMPLY UNTHINKABLE. THERE WILL NOT BE A **SECOND WORLD WAR**.

THIS INVENTION WILL PROTECT US FROM EVIL INTENTIONS AND IT WILL GUARANTEE A PEACEFUL FUTURE FOR HUMANITY.

MR. TESLA I THINK I MUST INTERRUPT YOU HERE, I HAVE ENOUGH MATERIAL TO WRITE A BOOK.

I REALLY APPRECIATE YOUR TIME...

AND I AM GRATEFUL FOR THIS OPPORTUNITY.

IT WAS A PLEASURE, GEORGE. WE CAN ORGANISE ANOTHER INTERVIEW ANYTIME YOU LIKE.

Chapter 14

> "As I review the events of my past life I realize how subtle are the influences that shape our destinies."

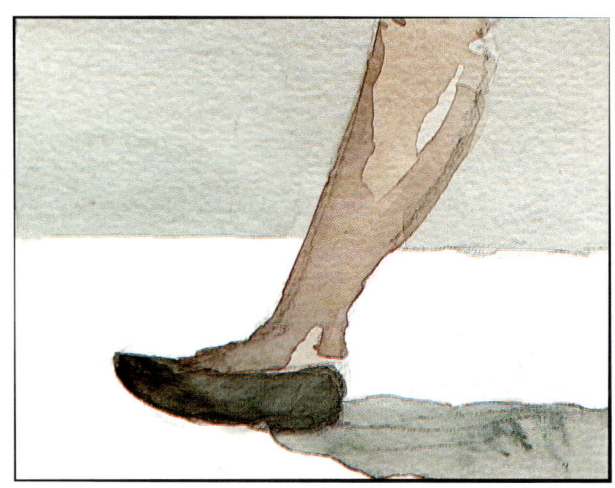

KNOCK KNOCK

(37) On 7th January 1943 Nikola Tesla was found dead at the age of 86 in his room 3327 at the Hotel Newyorker. All of his belongings were seized by the FBI and later analysed by the American electrical engineer, inventor, and physicist, John George Trump.

COPIES OF TESLA'S PAPERS CONCERNING **PARTICLE BEAM WEAPONRY (DEATH RAY)** WERE SENT TO **PATTERSON AIR FORCE BASE** IN **DAYTON, OHIO**. BASED ON TESLA'S DOCUMENTS, THE **U.S. AIR FORCE** CONDUCTED AN OPERATION NICK-NAMED **"PROJECT NICK"**. THE RESULTS WERE NEVER PUBLISHED AND TESLA'S PAPERS DISAPPEARED.

Chapter 15

> "Peace can only come as a natural consequence of universal enlightenment and merging of races, and we are still far from this blissful realization."

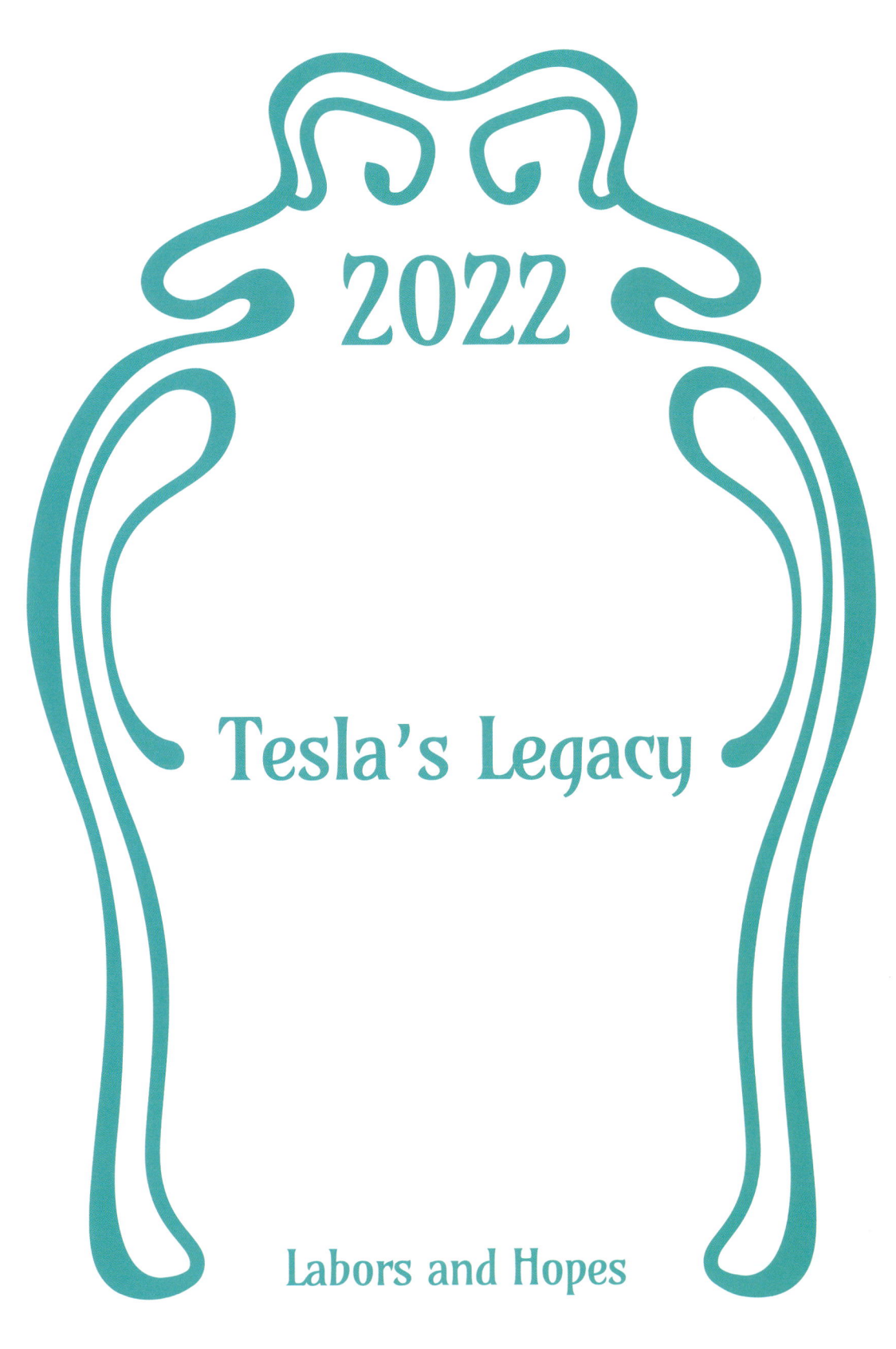

*"The scientific man does not aim at an immediate result.
He does not expect that his advanced ideas will readily be taken up.
His work is like that of a planter – for the future.
His duty is to lay the foundation for those who are to come and point the way.
He lives and labors and hopes".*

Nikola Tesla

Nikola Tesla left us a new kind of future.
He left us a future where we are encouraged to seek knowledge.
A future where we use his discoveries and improve upon them.

He pursued the complete mastery of mind over the material world, the harnessing of human nature for human needs.
He relentlessly pursued his dreams and allowed us to carry on dreaming, to communicate knowledge and exchange ideas.
He dreamt of a world where scientific breakthroughs would be celebrated, where they would be frontpage news, and today we are getting closer to achieving his dreams.

He dreamt of peace, he dreamt of a universe that provided us with energy and empowered us all.
Nikola Tesla, the man who defined our future, sought nothing for himself and left so much for us.

Nikola Tesla registered at least **308 patents** in **27 countries**, to protect a total of **125 inventions**.
In **1889**, he submitted a total of **37 applications** for his **polyphase system**.

IN THE EARLY **1950'S**, NIKOLA TESLA'S NEPHEW **SAVA KOSANOVIĆ** COLLECTED THOUSANDS OF HIS DOCUMENTS AND ITEMS AND SENT THEM TO **BELGRADE**, THE CAPITAL OF THE **SOCIALIST FEDERAL REPUBLIC OF YUGOSLAVIA.**

The Nikola Tesla Museum was opened on December 5th, 1952 and founded mostly on Sava Kosanović's collection.

Tesla's ashes arrived in Belgrade from the United States in 1957 and are kept in a golden spherical urn inside the museum.

A special Thanks to...

Abigail **Aharon Haravon** Alastair Mathews **Alba** Aleksandar Mrkić **Aleksandar Radulović** Alessandro Gori Alessandro Beltrame **Alex P** amijan **Ana Keserić** Ana Kušaković **Ana Marković** Ana Pajić Simović **Ana Stamenković** Andor Luhović **Andrea Pilia** Andrej Vukanović **Andy B Nicholson** Anica Đokić **Annika Vukanović** Antun Debak 3327.io **Atti** Berber Biala-Hettinga **Biagio Dall'Agnese (PG. 95 / 96 / 97)** Bojan Roško **Bojana Brankov** Bosko **Branimir & Vesna Kosovac** Branislava Gajić Stanojević **Branko Andrić** Caroline **Charles I.N. Venn** Chas Nelson **Chris Farmer** Dan Dalal **Darren** Dave Thurston **David Barco** David Jovanvoski **Davor Rostuhar** Dejan Tonić **Dejan Trajković** Deni **Dimitrije & Nevena Stamenković** DragonsDusk **Dušan Marković** Dušan Perić **Dušan Vujović** Dušica Brankov-Žikić **E. Quijano** Esel Design **Eva Werli** Evita **Fabio Franceschini & Ivana PG. 149 / 150 / 151** Filip Nemet **Gregory L DeLong** Hooloovoo Houghton Igor & Charlene Stamenković **Igor Spasić (PG. 153 / 154)** Igor Stojnov **Infostud Grupa** Istvan Balogh **Ivan Abraš Stamenković** Ivan Jovanović **Ivan Senić** Ivan Smolović **Jack Sisterson** Jan Kula **Janez Dovc** Jared Kinsfather **Jelena & Nemanja Ivančević** Jelena Popović Đorđević **Jelena Šaponjić** Jelena Todorović **Jonathan Naab** Jovana Ilijašević **Jovana Savić** Judy Lynn **Jules Kovačević** Justin J McNamara **Karen Small Gemin** Katharina Hoene **KEIN DESIGN** Kerber Games **KimBerry2021** Kitty Crab **Ksenija Milić** Lavender Brooke **Leonardo Spanu** Lorenzo Pilia **Lorna Swindley-Wilson** LOVE onlus **Magdalena Vukosavljević** Mamma **Marcela Krajcovicova** Marco Pilia **Marko Bežulj** Marko Govoruša **Marko Simić** Martin Avsenik **Matija Minović** Maurizio Montis **Mihaela** Milan Petrović **Mile Lukić** Miljan Rajković **Miloš Radulović** Miloš Stojković **Miloš Žikić** Miroslav Beseda **Neil Howie** Neila Rodriguez **Nellie Cole** Nenad Severović **Nicholas Kasić** Nicholas Trow **Nicola Giorgi** Niko Klansek **Nikola Đuza** Nikola Rudić **Nikolina Božanović** Nina Wade **Norbert Racsko** Olgica Zećević Stanojević **Olivera Petrović** Ola **Olja Dobroskok-Janković** Osvaldo Duilio Rossi **ozayr arnold** Pankaj Kapur **Pavle Ilijašević** Perry **Petar** Petar Bojović **Pierre Reljanović** Predrag Spasojević **Prince Eric Vickers** RAFFARK **Ragnarok Fans** Rob Baird **Rob Steinberger** Robert Yee **Ronald** Saioa Rodriguez **Samuel & Aurora Pita Costa** Sanja Beronja **Sasha** Sasho Razmoski **Sava** Sergey Kochergan **Sherlocked** Simon Mok **SlovoSla** Spomenka Petrović **Stan Smiljanić** Tanja & Fabian Vendrig **Tatiana Krivosheeva** Teodora Vujičić **The Creative Fund by BackerKit** Toki **Tom Magarian** Tomislav Perišić **Trevor Bibić** Uglješa Radulović **Ugnius Jakubelskas** Vanja & Milan Stamenković **Vera Werli** Vesna M **Vlad Jerca** Vlad Nešić **Vladan Anđus** Владимир Бојовић **Vladimir Radunović** Жика Ивановић **Zlatko Đorđević** Zoja Kukić **Zoran Janković**

"Of all things, I liked books best."
Nikola Tesla

CIP - Каталогизација у публикацији
Народна библиотека Србије, Београд

741.5:929 Тесла Н.

MEUCCI, Daniele, 1982-
   Nikola Tesla. The Man Who Defined the Future : A Grafic Novel by Daniele Meucci / [illustrations and storyboard author Daniele Meucci ; text authors Daniele Meucci, Branko Andrić, Chris Farmer]. - Beograd : Komshe, 2022 (Jagodina : Zlatna knjiga). - 196 str. : ilustr. ; 26 cm

Tiraž 2.000.

ISBN 978-86-86245-48-9

a) Тесла, Никола (1856-1943)

COBISS.SR-ID 63577865